NOT YET *but* STILL

NOT YET *but* STILL

MARGARET AVISON

LANCELOT PRESS
Hantsport, Nova Scotia

Cover design by Kate Jackson

ISBN 0-88999-619-9
Published 1997

THE CANADA COUNCIL | LE CONSEIL DES ARTS
FOR THE ARTS | DU CANADA
SINCE 1957 | DEPUIS 1957

The publisher acknowledges the support of the Canada Council for the Arts for our publishing program.

We also acknowledge the assistance of the Nova Scotia Department of Education.

LANCELOT PRESS LIMITED, Hantsport, Nova Scotia
Office and production facility located on Hwy. No. 1, 1/2 mile east of Hantsport

4

CONTENTS

ACKNOWLEDGEMENTS   8

LOOKING OUT
Old Woman At a Winter Window   13
Beyond Weather, or From a Train Window   14
From Now — On?   15
Contemplative Hour   17
Lit Sky and Foundered Earth   18
Thought In A Sick-Room   19
Not Quite Silently   20

BEING OUT
Slow Advance   25
There Are No Words For   27
When Their Little Girl Had Just Died   28
When The Bough Breaks   29
Knowing The New   30
Sultry Day   31
asap; etc.   32
Making A Living   33
Air and Blood   34
Late Perspective   36
"Tell Them Everything That I Command You;
    Do Not Omit A Word"   37
We Are Not Desecrators   38
Potentiality   40

NOW
A Peculiarity: Local Loyalties   43
A Basis   44
Music Was In The Wind   47

Communication At Mortal Risk   49
Poring   50
Artless Art   51
Transition   52
Cross-Cultural, or, Towards Burnout   53
Cultures Far and Here   56
The Risk Of No Communication   58
Family Members   60
A Women's Poem: Now   61
A Women's Poem: Then and Now   62
Aftermath of Rebellion   63
For a Salty and Sainted Friend in her 90's   65
Seer, Seeing   66
How Open, Who Are Compassed Here?   70

WHO
Concert   73
The Familiar Friend, But By The Ottawa River   74
Astonishing Reversal   76
In Season and Out Of Season   77
To Counter Malthus   80
And If No Ram Appear   81
What John Saw   82
Prodded Out Of Prayer   84
Embrace Change?   85
Breath Catching   86
Proving   87

HIGH DAYS
Christmas Doubts Dissolved   91
Two Perilous Possibilities   92
That Friday — Good?   94
Interim   95

"One Rule Of Modesty and Soberness"   96
It Isn't Really True?   100

FOR THE FUN OF IT
A Seed Of History   105
Word: Russets   106
Shelter?   107
A Kept Secret   108
Resting On A Dry Log, Park Bench, Boulder   109
News Item   111
Instrumentalists Rehearse   112
Three Bears   113

***JOB*: WORD AND ACTION**
Confrontation and Resolution, In *Job*   117

ACKNOWLEDGEMENTS

As before, I want to thank Joan Eichner. She has been a consistent encourager, and has helped me to stop and re-read, and then revise! Without her prodding, the scrambled papers on and around the desk would never have been assembled into a manuscript. And I am grateful to Kate Jackson for agreeing to design the cover.

Also I would like to acknowledge the first publication of some of these poems, in: *Compass, Ellipse, Journal of Canadian Poetry, The New Quarterly, Poetry Canada, Presbyterian Record, Queen's Quarterly;* and in the "New Poems" section of *Selected Poems* (1991), Oxford University Press.

"The sun a cataract in a blinding sky..."

Eli Mandel

LOOKING OUT

Old Woman At a Winter Window

From squared-off quarters
through a frosted pane
I stare into the glittering
quartz of the air, marbled with
tiny streamers from
valiant chimneys down along the valley.

It is as if we pit ourselves
against a congealing It.
We claim these square ceiling and walls
and floor from the immensity
as all that have, for us,
meaning, against the encroaching ice,

the ice that somehow
signals another space, a fearful,
glorious amplitude.

Beyond Weather, or *From a Train Window*

Snowflakes in starlight, obliterated into
weft and stippling, buried under
combed sweep and depth, month upon month,
crusting and powdered over,
now — in the gloaming fields — become
round little pools
bright with the lift of the sky they left last autumn.

Mineral beauty. Most such is still
long, for long, hidden.

From Now — On?

The family car has come
for the son who believed
he had left home.
His college luggage heaved
into the back too leaves,
with two of them, still room
in the front seat for him.

Is it his last year?
Where are his companions
to gather and conspire
falsely about reunions?
It's good there's no-one there
to witness these old tensions,
old bonds, new fear.

The future closes down
with the slammed trunk.
Dazed by distractions
and like a drunk
awash suddenly with affection
and close to tears, he thinks
of the long-lost home town.

For him, is this disruption?
"An end and no beginning"
now his life's caption?
Ice on bright puddles, birds all singing
to mock the nothingness suction,
the spiritless direction,
his flattened pinions?

In the vague inattention of a too
long life, out walking by
that college: how
many spring term-ends have I
seen the cars load, the shy
parents reclaiming their boy.
And this "how many" is also,
for me, disruption.

Contemplative Hour

Is there a precious stone somewhere between
pearl-pale and Peace-Rose-colour?
not matte, but only subtly
reflecting light?

It is first light.
The quiet lake four miles away
breathes fragrant peace to this
hill window.
Breathes, not reflects.

Who or what can be
a lake to light, when dark
still muffles the sorrowful thoroughfares?
when worlds of people huddle
heaped up alongside water, everywhere
land once heaved up out of water?

Cities want more window — both to see
and be — though in this last of time,
this early April day
is precious, and not stone.

Lit Sky and Foundered Earth

The nighthawk? no, a gull
far off, only affirms
the quiet of this hour,
as do the children's cries
in the near-dark — still playing,
guilty with freedom, after
this sudden summer on a
school day in October.
Hearing them, you know how
flushed their faces, how
desperate for one last dare:
they listen too for that
voice from a lit window or doorway
to beam them down, and in.

Thought In a Sick-Room

Single leaf shadow
touches leaf
in the still morning window.

The branches of
young leaves (outdoors)
shimmer.

In the eclipse, when I was very young,
someone said — I was a city child —
"Watch it on the pavement
under a big old tree."

It's true.
Beyond the dot and dash of
less leafy trees
find one in lofted fullness
and the light, in perfect
little sun-round shadows of
itself, falls
on the bald earth — or, in eclipses,
little sun-crescents.

Not Quite Silently

What light of a snow-cloud
here, among us, from where we
stumble along
to as dim far out into the void
as seeing can believe,
can be so overshadowed?

Pale diagrams of snowy
roof levels, and roof angles
rise up out of the smudge
of crouched buildings and
tree-tangle.

The once familiar small things
(normally part of
anybody's day)
blur into the fading of
hill and valley. This
somehow
gives all we know a face and
being, though

all, all are muffled, moved
under, moved down into themselves; down
into the unknowable
earth of us all.

Though light is overshadowed, yet the far
comes close, the unknowable
near; the random usual "here"
is sifted down

feathering eyelid, lashes, blank
eyeball, as if with holy
fear.

Being Out

Slow Advance

One of those tall tall birds
but puce (not
pink as flamingos' pictures are),
high stepping,
      through what seemed the detritus
      of all my city lanes and childhood vacant
      lots — a shadow-casting
collage of grasses, other (one-legged) people's
wet socks, odd machine-scraps and
glass fragments —
among a few small inky
patches of rainwater,
draped his slow knee-to-toe
tall tall legs
forward, one by

one. His progress
seemed more significant than memory.

A freshening breeze
teased his shoulder feathers, his
north-sky-coloured shoulders.

More to report would be invention.

Slow, moving, but
with no significant progress,
no furrowing take-off, ponderous
wing-flapping — was it
the dream-reversal of frenetic motion?

For me in my involvement there
perhaps.
But the deliberate purposefulness
of that tall tall
bird was absolute.
Is not a dream.

There Are No Words For

when there are no words:

— — —

the sweat and clench
of his crescendoing pain
you, helpless, cannot know.

Two together
each quite alone.

Joy too
can single out.
Yes; it aches to be, nonetheless,
always wider in radiance.

Audiences there are
for pain and joy;
some, cold but fascinated,
have comments;
most are involved   look on
helplessly   but
they have no words — even not
for you,
remembering oneness but now frozen out by
that odd proscenium,
privacy,   respected.

Having no words is not
safe. It is
then the only good.

When Their Little Girl Had Just Died

Does pain prise people apart?
It can.
Who cranks the wedge wider?
No one.
None can give counsel re the split
to two, lopped so, inert,
who shrink from double hurt
(worse, none).

O ocean of known pain
engulph, then, overwhelm
these two into absorption
past all cataclysm
beneath that far pacific line
where pain and joy are one.

When The Bough Breaks

Though through the early murk
   the sun, a tangerine ball,
       bulged, briefly,
   the sultry dearth of all
   but gray and remote glower
   is all we're left with.

Soapstone massaged by the faint
   motion of my slowest moving,
I pass a scraggly man
on a park bench, solidly intent
on a black Bible —
       triangled, knees to eyes.
A Chinese grandmother
loiters among 22 pigeons on a
glum little square.

City seems loath to stir.
Even the lemon lilies wanly
feel for their little day as if
   it were not now.

Knowing The New

The detritus of winter is
hollowed to the rind. But
we find, one day, those old
ridges have vanished, are
washed clean away.

Then for awhile
straining anticipation flounders
as every day follows chill day — those
brooding snappish days.

They have passed. Now
even in the city, breezes
are gentle with that moist
earth smell.

Suddenly utterance is everywhere.
Little new leaves are
blossomy in frills and lace under the
limpid blue.
And the magnolia has
haloed high around itself a dome
of space,
an eloquent soundlessness
the birds can understand and
re-voice for the wide world.

Sultry Day

It smells like glue.
The bus windows give on
carsheds and
abandoned storefronts.
We do keep breathing
though this vile air.

Pressures are drawing in
however.

Soon there will rise
a sulphur and violet sky.
It will convulse in
fire and water.

Then, with the soiled old world
hosed clean, the blue
windows of light will be
clear, the air
cedar-tip sweet.

asap; etc.

Acronyms, alas,
become words-without-etymology;
components crumble blind;
the agglomerating initials find
themselves picked up by ear without apology
by those too used to symbols without mass.

Are moon and foreheads, and this opening rose
(massively present), nonetheless
the cryptic relics of one word
we know no way to now? have heard
of only in distress
from some original who chose

to spot particulars as part
of utterance, acronymic,
not conceived as final? Sense
and sound of the immense?
fully articulate in a tongue untaught?

Well, that's a place to start.

Making A Living

The industrious young
as if as well carefree
run here at sandpiper gait,
     with the weight of the earth or the
     wavering line of the foam
     from an alien element
     sketching a scalloping path:
they veer and flee and come running
busily, as if carefree.

The old stand hunched,
motionless, like a morning
heron on mist-smoking water standing,
     the way a lightning-crippled oak
     mimicking lightning in its
     old blasted branches
     seems forever bereft of leafing.
Earth under water, sky over all,
waiting; though
there will be, abruptly, a
brief tussle: life, from death.
Another fast is broken.

Air and Blood

The beautiful Tuesday morning
light is refined by the
haze of
metropolis, breathing.

Away out there in the pitiless
clarity of field and riverflats,
one by one, in an odd
kind of despair,
countrymen, the young, torn but
compelled, throw off
pitchfork and pieties,
shoulder belongings, hit the road.

The bus slews to a gravelly stop
just up the grade. He runs,
bundle joggling. Aboard
is the metropolis's
breathing, but not here
refined.

From private acres, near and far away,
somehow a diaphragm seems to be in an
agglomerative rhythmic
tilting, dislodging, sloughing off.

Now!

Feverish, at first
exhilarating, seems
the energy,

the beauty even —
as, on this beautiful Tuesday, morning
light is refined by
the haze of megalopolis, breathing.

Late Perspective

Ribbed sand under clear shallows,
   stray, shadow-probing pebbles,
      receive the quiet light.

Changed
     since under the soundless
   weight borne deep under ocean,
   the boil and hiss, and there
   sealed off, hardened, still
   unresisting, massively shouldered out
   and moved by those
   terrible forces that grind
   down, grind down,
this shore-pan suffers now the mild
face of the morning.

Long we stand listening here.

Then the children are brought and quickly
prancing up shells of water, they
muddle the parallel patterns of the sand
along the stippled shallows,
reckless — why should they not be? — of the ancient
touches that grit on their
spade handles, their
tender ankle skin,

and eons' flow slows to the
intermittent droplets of
their morning's timeless time.

"Tell Them Everything
That I Command You;
Do Not Omit A Word"
(Jer. 26:2b)

Night? barely past noon?
An eerie quiet, then
the crack and rustle of fear.

But in that hour
just before the storm/doom
crashed down,

with force and immediacy, heard
by every child, woman and man,
came the word, spoken
through Jeremiah who
moved past darkness.

Yes, they had heard
his long-range forecasts.
But now, they knew, believing now
had them closed in with seeing.

We Are Not Desecrators

After a noisy night of rain
sun comes flooding. Droplets shine
on every blade of grass and curl of budding
leaf. Under the young
maples, under the cloud and sunpour,
tree-meal spreads its saffron glow.

Silenced almost is the city's endless
snoring, our kettle-drum activity
(one playing field away).

My kind out there sullies
it all, as I do being here.

Yet we, providing an unlikely
context for miracle, maybe, alone,
are inwardly kindled.
(The songsparrows, for instance, are
wholly given to improvising their
immemorial singing — further
compelling us despoilers
to pure awareness!)

Also, the night was no surprise.
This morning, with its opening skies,
is.

Through the preempted hours
and all our outs and ins, there stir
long-lost rememberings

of sudden summer. New
antiphonal vistas open.

Potentiality

Humble is the intensity of
a seed.

It lies there
too small to cast a shadow,

as the invisible is too large, compassing
light and shadow both;   .

yet there is
a bond that makes them one.

Now

A Peculiarity: Local Loyalties

If only I were a farmer
I would put this better. But

suppose a salesman drives in and
strolls around to find
where you are working, and sees
your ripening apples, the aging
trees (but sturdy)
(the young orchard is all
spindle and tracery still),
and says:

"This product we prepare
from our own research
will swell your fruit by four
times, and redden its cheek
to make it more enticing
to the public."

                      You stand listening.

Your dad once said,
"Son, never trade
flavour for show.
Offer something choice.
Fewer may want it, but in the course
of giving them quality you're giving
yourself incentive, and satisfaction —
just about enough, at the day's end."

So you clear your throat, and send
him away with a shrug, and an apple in his hand.

A Basis

Preface. This is about
many of us. You deride
the stereotype of my peculiar
sub-culture? That would be good-
bye to something you might want understood.

The missionary "call"
is part expulsiveness.
In all, in Antioch,
stresses through Paul, the saint
(despite that gentle "encourager" on his team)
may have begun to fray a seam or two.
They, moved to send them out,
welcomed the Spirit's "Go",
thankfully left on their own then, to "work out
their own salvation", having forced themselves to
"go" themselves in order to stay.

Am I accusing Paul
of a short fuse? of chafing
on a short leash? Was he
a venturesome unsettler? Where he went,
restlessly, on and on,
his stays established outposts of the
heavenly imperium which must
in turn disrupt all empires. Saints galore
experienced then the senders'
stresses, unsettlings, frayed seams;
but also they experienced
the saint's propulsive
fire in the bones, although operative

in followers now; the leader
first demonstrated and then
taught and, yes, enforced
following as his
own freedom, and as theirs — and ours.

So an expulsive Paul
was after all the heartbeat of heaven's purposes?
But was the hard-driven church
in Antioch at fault?
Was the word ("Send forth!")
mistranslated in some of their hearts
as "let's get rid of"; a prayer even: "Relieve
us of the gad-
fly in our sweetest ointment?   Leave,"
perhaps they thought, "that we may live
sheltered but no more driven by our faith."

Faraway saints become dear to
the here unthreatened.

Most threads are twisted.
They tend to knot. I.e. the best
must be, on earth,
only the worst in course of
being transfigured.

——————

Disruptive change could not
be hindered.
Nor can it. Surrendered to
impulse some venturers may go

alien ways — were these galling at home?
    Expelled?   Sent?   Summoned?

The outcome is the same,
there and even here.

Music Was in the Wind

It was Orpheus all along!
He carried Eurydice down, down
into the earth
in his arms, going himself with her
since this was the only way
out of her mortal maze now.
All he had then he risked
except a love strong and steady enough
never to share her
relief in this fine-sifted silence, nor
her torn
loyalties to this private place
and to the devastated but remembered
home where she was known.

First it had to be down.
He was no
stoic, no ascetic, moved to
goodness without experience
of all our billion moments. Did he
hear what the shepherds overheard?
sweet singing in the choir?

He carried her he loved
the whole way down.

The strange travail home
up into light
emptied his arms. He
took her by the hand, and she was walking.
And on the way they would be

sometimes sensitive to a loss as she
lived it out in a familiar
and yet an altered world,
remembering a morning, in a song,
going about the city in the streets,
yet even then
knowing him once again beyond our wall:
"Arise, and come...."

Communication at Mortal Risk

The prow of that icebreaker
was a person.

The channel is still open.
It must be kept so.

Another person is already
in place. Others
are primed.

> *Surely this deadly rescue*
> *must not go on.*

This channel is our
local concern;
there are others even
more, or as, vital;

these concern us
deeply too. But here we must
keep at it while
someone still can.

Poring

These words* become
opaque when wrestled down.
They're plain but ponderous
with pastness.

Yet there begins to
emerge — see! — far,
farther: a distinct design,
like miniature landscapes in the sun
out through the arch in a Gozzoli
painting.

Out of the numbing
pastness opens an — escape!
an invitation? One expects
to breathe that light
somehow, and perhaps see
even the grassblades, and the
shadows of the grassblades.

---

* E.g., in Leviticus

Artless Art

When we were children, who
did not contrive
a secret language? — nobody "else" to know
the key, for ever.

By now
both of us have, I guess,
written it out
plain, in the common tongue. We
know, though, that the secure
never will decipher it.

But to one another we,
here and there, are known,
all marvelling at the
how-it-is-said
so that the what
still scarcely matters.

Transition

When they ransacked
the ancient memory
some became learned
and the learning became dust;
some would have bartered
their loot. But
found out in the market
it had all
become fools' gold.

The hollowed ancient places
echoed with silences.

The tension rises
through the snowlight of the
dark hours. Cut off.
And listening past
possibilities.

Odd, that such yearning wonder
should, for fear
turn to ice.

Cross-Cultural, or, *Towards Burnout*

Your rage is bearable as your
swallowed insults and the limp
collusion with us were not
to you, were to us echoes only of
our unauthentic guilt.

Yet your rage hurts.
A post-colonial white woman, I am
therefore a thing-hog,
easy taker-for-granted, helpless
to unmake the bed
others made for me, even before
grandpa (and even he was
simply another fellow working long hours,
kindly, respectful, whether paid or not).
And I lie, tossing, in that
incontestably comfortable bed.

What has been crafted in behind
green hedges of "our heritage"
took centuries, took lives.
It formalized, in time, our
savage sorrow into this
chamber music. We need
a life half-lived-out, maybe more
to be constrained to music in
quiet fullness of sorrow.

We are outraged at your
raw grief, at
the bony barricades of

borne indignity:
your five-year-old coming in,
defeated, facing still
another day of what
our five-year-old will say and do.

Through Jeremiah I had
faced up to God's fierce anger.

Therefore your rage is the
long held under
knowledge of the holy child's
knowledge of
the spittle, the
flogged back, the suave
manipulator's deathly mockery,
present, every wracked
generation, as if helplessly.

Your work is dark and bitter.

Ours, rounded up at last from the
once fortress city, picking our way
out through its rubble, bound
for forced labour in remote Asian
cities, or
slavery in
others' mansions and palaces.

Our God endures.

The sentinel trees
on a far hilly ridge

remind us of perennial
destruction, restoration, on
wave lengths much too vast to ease
you and the child today
or us into tomorrow.

Cultures Far and Here

or rich and poor?

One voice, one looming face, first,
one floor and roof,
windows on daylight, and (when the
wonder must be tracked)
out in the windy grass
or along cliffs,
or through the steamy lowlands
I've never seen, with leaves
as large as elephant ears,
or in a secret cove
safe from the thundering surf —

these and the strangeness
of meeting a potential friend
with different memories
to travel with,
and others, more, confronting sometimes:

all these early imprintings give us
person by person
our natures, each unique as fingerprints.

That's frightening. We cluster
telling each other
stories that build the vault of a
shelter from the wholly
unknown, comforted by what
is recognizable in our overlapping
awareness.

But sky and weather
have a way of disregarding our
walls, sweeping us on to
not being an "us".

Out there it's larger
every time we're stripped
of almost everything familiar.

If it were violent exposure
it would be less
insidious. Because it's featureless
the wide starless daylight is
vacuous.

East-west, equator-outwards, people
scramble like flotsam, and the tides
wash out all little dunes and bays and
private promontories.

The Risk of No Communication

"X" — "To 'interface' I'll go
out under rainstripped trees
among the ones who
hurl up their sticks and choose
the shiniest chestnuts, squinting at the sky.

"Or in the amber city go
among the fruitstalls and the cheese
markets, mashing down the
greens and sawdust on the walkways,
alert for the particular face
never before, nor since, seen, open,
even responsively human
for an instant, as we carry our
different faces on into
each his own life."

    "A" — "No. No. To interface
       is to bring the parties' two
       predicates to contrive a
       single new
       composite terminology.
       The mix may spur
       ideas, shift perspectives, even
       highlight some overlooked potentiality."

"X" — "A factoring down?
Cutting mutual losses? never
facing one another?
(Face. Faces. Etymology:
'face' — "a making", *cf* 'sur-faces')."

"X"'s younger friend — "Such Latin roots
have become marginal. What roots
nurture the dessication of language now?
with wires as good as stems?
Structure will be secure in their
designing hands."

Family Members

The tethered dory thuds
in its lonely sarabande
after the speedboat's passing.
Thuds on the dock, as gradually
criss-crossing wavelets
scallop the weathered piles.
Thud. Then bump. Then nudge.

Wood shaped to shel-
ter even the clumsiest oarsman,
shaped to cumber
the sundanced waters or
the still angora mists of dawn.
Wood of the dock, wet fibering
wood piles solid on rock
fixed in cement — knee-deep
in a dry autumn, hipdeep and standing steady
when March foments the slush to gnaw
and no one sees or listens.

Wood, tied to wood,
but not by wood and
only in waiting intervals;
each mostly on its own.

A Women's Poem: Now

Women are breadwinners perforce
when their pay is their sole resource.
Or when couples aspire to arrive
at a house — not a cell in a hive.

Santa Lucia was practical
too. Only after betrothal
to a rich man did she share her
dowry, all of it, with the poor.

Someone (her husband?) suspected
her Christ-act, and to correct it
let the Roman prosecutor
pursue the matter, and martyr her.

A Women's Poem: Then and Now

Some people couldn't care less
how they dress.
A few resolve to wear
only what was someone else's before.

Most people like to shop.
They never stop
and smile if something fits — and is reduced.
They buy the mass-produced.

One or two let salons present
them well, for each event,
uncaring about cost, keeping in mind
that theirs is one-of-a-kind.

In this new age the fashion
is wearing a used person.
An emperor's clothes, in artless ostentation?
Why "reincarnation?"

Why contemplate it, over
a name, unique, forever?
Before opting for evil — and shame and flight —
Adam and Eve went naked in the full light!

Aftermath of Rebellion

When runners came with news
after the Battle in the Forest
the King's hopes stirred — here was
no rout, no loyal remnant
straggling home to defend
an indefensible throne.

Yes, the first praised the Lord his God
(the King's), obviously glad in
the monarch and his kingdom
made secure. Yet
(and hope flickered):
"What of Absalom?"

The second, the official slower
runner, with a word
stifled the air and
hope went out.

"Would God that *I* had died for *him*."

The father's lament
has lingered on the ancient air of grief
at least till now.

A vain, muscular, risk-defying,
fine-looking heir to
prospects that one day would
amaze the Queen of Sheba,
a rebel, a contemptuous
underminer, had flung off

— forever now —
in his young man's euphoria,
his father's hand.

For such a delinquent
even, a sovereign, sick at heart
learned what it is when
a father loves.

For a Salty and Sainted Friend in her 90's

She had survived Intensive Care
but still valiantly hoped
to escape hospital or what-
ever new way-station,
e.g. a nursing-home.

"It saved your life," said the doctor.
"Saved — from what?" She
wryly rebukes his jauntiness
at having intervened. Her eyes are
snapping with conviction and —
amusement.
Almost disdainful of death, she
presses him,   "From what?"

"No," her granddaughter
gently puts in,
"not from, saved for
another not-too-difficult
year or so perhaps? or for
mornings like this, quiet, with the
lilac and white lilac
dimness of it? for
some unpredictable ...?

Well maybe (grudgingly
conceded). But, "Saved —
for what?" And let
the lady answer.

Seer , Seeing

I am no cow of Bashan, Amos.
No. I'm not poor, for all I've tried to end up
understanding that, by being it.
It didn't work. I work.
My meals are
ordinary, and by no means
easily shared in
fact — though gestures can
make maybe some
trifling difference somewhere.

The scale is huge now, but
the story still the same,
all this more-than-millenium later.

It's hemispherics we talk now
or off and on emergency relief
(we're bothered, even generous.)
Our "world" still has
palaces, malls, temples, doogoodery
and makegoodery — institutionalized.

Institutions have all the words, but
there's not an institution speaks for
you, or for me hearkening for you,
any more than for

her, left alive, with listening eyes
sitting amid a strew of
bodies where a passing gust
ruffles, idly.

These were that "other half"
that is no longer half a world away.

We worked for, dreamed for, this;
        or worked to live, and ended building this
structure, made from traditional
materials of the first excellence.
What is your quarrel, Amos?

        Tear down
        Tear down.

They will? We?
Institutions rainbowed like soapsuds
in bonny air are bursting, superseded
by predators
out to hunt down the all too much that
is no more.

You fulminate, released to
sweep all before the
tides of holy anger.

Then, Amos, you end up with
bucolic bliss!

        As though perennial contentment
        were bedded down on everyone
        else's fetid
        declension into formlessness!

        Din into my ears
        your dirge, Amos. Set my last

gaze on
a whole people convulsed, roam where they
may,
horizon to horizon to horizon.

I cannot yet
see, my vision blurred by vapour trails,
riot-torn cities' smoke,
hot breathings from cored mountains,
oh, by the too-late industries
      puncturing pre-sunset smog
      seeking too late to trans-
      mogrify tropical and
      other swarming nowheres to
      spitefully replicate club men and
      women and their
      clubs and memories.
And yet I see you
      banking on seed and
embers and all through
      the world of bombast and
      frozen-eyed bewilderment,
      and torn inside too
      by your own torrent of words,
      all through, you resolutely breathed in
      sun and rain's sweetness
      with simple joy,

      and not just in that
      curious coda, that halcyon aftermath,

but all through, all the way through
with a true hunger banking on

one sturdy today
until tomorrow is today, until
the one with no tomorrow.

How   Open,   Who Are Compassed Here?

Guessing what the world
will be when we
develop multi-faceted
eyes, like flies',
unsteadies its slow girth
sweeping from west
to east, trailing its
skies.

WHO

Concert

Learning, I more and more
long for that simplicity,
clarity, that willingness
to speak (from anonymity...)
all those impenetrables, when words
are more like bluebell petals under
an absorbed heaven.

You fret because the underbrush
is dense, the way uncleared it seems
where you now find yourself?

Words have been given. Once.
Words that are storm and sun and rain.
Listening earth, where they have fallen
finds seed casings begin
to split,
roots throb. As though
some unimaginable response is
implicit in that speaking.

Fulfilment is in promise
and still more resonant longing.

The Familiar Friend*, But By The Ottawa River

River, enriched in the last light:
this is the cool of the day.
Calm and close, all together,
noone needs words, the
stillness brimming, like those
muscular waters in the lingering light.

And did I plan
before you chose to come?
or after, for that matter, when we were
at peace, breathing companionability
together?
But there were fleeting
expressions, wordless mealtimes
and I could know that that
uninterrupted unemphatic
walking the roads, the hills, would generate
exasperated wonder-
ing about something ... else,
before the marking of time
(and it was sure), somebody ...
else who would
not be all-encompassing.

I knew I am the one
you one day, towards

* The person addressed is Judas Iscariot. The words cen-
turies later reflect a possible train of thought in the human
mind of his human-divine friend whom he would betray. And
die of it.

evening, would
leave. You had prepared for
what had to happen.

When it did it burned
deeper than your mind.
Nothing will medicine the sore
but an abiding with the wordless glory —
mirroring waters flowing.

If only memory were not
one function of mind.

Astonishing Reversal

In holiness alone
is freedom.

My skeins come twisted to
my hands — I see
another's frayed;   tangled
too much to not be broken.

The holy one, who seemed to
put us all in constraint
by being —
why! all along —
will not be banished from
room or field or cockpit or
anywhere we are, is

patiently, alone,
fingering the snarls and
stringing out the one by one
way of liberation.

In Season and Out of Season

Today the blueness burns
inbetween new greens and space's
soundless blackness.
Yet we even now
discern more, cry:
No, lovely as May is
we would hear more.

> Moses, you are the voice
> the Voice spoke with.
> Centuries have not, will not,
> still that, therefore. The marvel
> of the pitched cradle of reeds, the appeal
> to a ruler-murderer's daughter's
> mothering heart, the barter
> of true for foster care that became both;
> your growing,
> that unexceptional miracle
> of years: it all made way for
> what? One small pure drop —
> anticipation? hope? — hung on life's
> strange leaf-edge; trembling in the light
> for years, for all your years indeed,
> for "By faith Moses ...".* It is said.

Exult in warmth and depth
of branches here? Yes, and yet Antarctica
in this same season,
snarls, pounces, gnaws — even while

---

* Heb. 11:24

today the earth
rejoices in deliverance in this zone.

Moses, your early privilege turned
when you saw abuse into
an alienating cause? What burned
was not the authorities' heartless
indignation, not
the mute slaves', not
even your own
violent indignation, in the end.
Bare-soled on desert sand
you bowed,
and bartered with your seclusion for
your people's whole concern,
the Other's deep concern,
finally given to both.

For many days
here, a sagging cloud and stiff
dark mat of branch and twig,
clacking, entombed us all. Now that winter's over
the trees and shrubs are thimbleberried with
chestnut flowers, with deep-breathed lilacs.

Moses, how does your solitary death —
and you went up the lonely crags
as bidden —
follow? Did the Voice
seek silence then? from faith
were you led ... further?
It may be heaven is the
light that ... conceals?

Your longing then was
not so much to
realize the Land for you were
sure about the Land
long since by faith,
but to be brought
where the celestial Other would
be known in fullness
however dark?

He saw the Lord. He, Moses, was seen
transfigured too, in mountain light, when
much was made plain by once
caring enough to pray to be
blotted out.
(For he had stood among his
fractious protesting people; he
recognized too his own
moment of failure to
stand with the Voice, heeding instead
an unholy flare of
exasperated nature. Once. Enough.)

Not in season, in the revolving
solar system, in which we turn
changeably, always.
Not without the appalling
lightless depth. Not but as a way station
perhaps   is the
unimaginable light where
all maybe is plain.

To Counter Malthus

None of us in this so
burdened earth has known
how to live, let alone
who is too many.

Presence, each day
afresh, you give a
purifying signal to
sting us alive.

Vast territories and seashores
still bear these thronging
strangers. May none die
without somebody caring.

To know even one other is
costly. And being known.
Alive, among so many
more now? a concern ...

Hunger makes men desperate, threatens
to congeal the quandary. Yet
Presence abides untouched
in the churn of Quantity.

And If No Ram Appear (Gen. 22:13)

I saw a father fudge on his first love
when a loved child,
  born in a family of faith
  in a world no longer in sympathy,
  born of an ancient lineage —
  only a stigma, here —
mattered more, in a moment of decision.

John 3:16
sang out, suddenly:
the only-begotten yielded up, the father
steadied by a harshly
beautiful, and implicit, priority,
with his whole heart
willing:

  goodness made real on earth,
  put within possibility, so that,
  by choice, an answering love
  could make complete the circuit. Shame became
  resplendence
for the priority stands.

Break open every sin of ours
this way! from a broken heart
forgiveness opens out,
more, finding
we matter. And how much.

*What John Saw**

The black holes out there, of pure (physical) force
in the heavens,
those in-and-out plosions, focused,
remote, in a rhythm of
incomprehensible infrequency
but nonetheless in time,
speak the extremes absolute of a rhythm
we mortals know.
They are like us contained in
creation's "Let it be so."

Who can comprehend, with a heart hungry
for meaning?
who does not feel the uprooting
tremor of one event —
one person's, or, in the stupefying
astronomers' book of hours, one
pulse of the megalorhythm?

Yes yes I know
this bronzing beech tree, the
blackening myrtle at its foot
(event in all my seasons,
seasoned for this long before I was
born) exists in a mere
twitch, is rushing towards the node
millennia away, and that just one

---

* Revelation 4

of many, just one episode.
Time curls on itself.

Least moments given, though,
can open onto
John's comprehender: here,
there, then, always
now, because unchanging, who
made light and ponderous rhythms, time, and all
pulsing particulars.
John saw him rainbowed in glory —
compact of all our music, hearing the farthest
compositions, and the most intricately
present. Magnet. Intensifier. Agonizingly
rediscovering, in shards, the shapes
design is satisfied to see.
One. White. Whole.

Secret within
all that John saw
is the bronzing beech tree
of this October twilight
though I do not yet see,
even in mind, being
not yet out of time.

Prodded Out of Prayer

Stilled yet by
the gauzed withdrawingness of
midmorning sky:

lo, a sharply lit
acutely poignant
and wonderfully humourous
vision.

It was an ant
towing a grass-blade
in a bee-line, but on
rougher terrain,
to the anthill.

Embrace Change?

Embrace? But he will
never draw near for long, would never
choose to pause here.

All right, all right,
I'm panicking.
           He's at my door.

Am I a
recommended B and B?

And though the door
opens only as far
as the chain, through the toe-edge
in the last light, I see
too much of elsewhere to be safe.

Shivering, I say no.
And he says nothing as he turns away.

Breath Catching

The one day will require
all times to be full.
There are no corners.
A beloved stranger
has gone
whose reappearing
spells apprehension, panic,
all we have to hang onto.

Proving

"... do not omit a word" (Jer. 26:2b)

Truth speaks
all things into being.
No word more, but
not one left unspoken.
Truth carves, incises,
to the bone,
and between bone and marrow.
No wonder
we want none of him.
The wonder is
truth loves;
died of it, once.

Truth lives.
Acting on what is spoken,
not a syllable extra,
nothing omitted,
brings into being
just what is prophesied.
That is the test —
not of what has been spoken
but for the hearer,
his act.

HIGH DAYS

Christmas Doubts Dissolved

The mayfly's day is significant for
God and that mayfly,
and mine yours his hers
to God, and each such 'me'.

God's little bodily birth is
absolutely unique,
distinct from what he chose
as our particularity.
It's in one flick of time's eternal eye
known, but not evidentiable
(there's what his mother told the
historian years later, but even he
traces a patrilinear descent —
having declared the virgin's miracle).

Were it all otherwise
would the point be, for the mayfly,
and for me, so
poignantly permanently new?

Two Perilous Possibilities

He was a discard, "bearing the disgrace."

Graciously (me too in the raggle-taggle)
summoned to join him there, we're set to "praise
continually". That is our "sacrifice"
bringing to equipoise his shame.

This on a drizzly December
midday staggers belief. Cement trucks lumber
past, on a muddy street.
Crowds jumble by, their faces
preoccupied, or strained, or smiling oddly, some
numbly conditioned to hurt. The number
of us, just in itself, disheartens from
crediting supernova-to-small-town-Alberta
focus on one
or the required crescendo
of that much "praising"
one by one.

But he is there still "bearing the disgrace."

Is this perhaps the day before — his table-
settings in place — he will summon
us the street people, us the straggle
of refugees and buskers and all
odds and sods — since thus
honoured guests are provided
his way? The preferred guests
whom we had honored

had to be superseded (for,
they said, their own sakes.)

Or is it still December
before again a new
genesis for one of us
because the focus still is on
one in "disgrace"
risking the end truly to
make it new?

That Friday — Good?

At least the twentieth century is ending.

Wretched   insignificant
hurt-all-over   all-through
is all there is.
Alone in the universe

and even then (feebly) the "Why?"

      Someone, if present,
      would make it go back to before
      or at least make it better?

That's not true.

Abandoned.

      What if the someone
      were to be, every sinking moment,
      were to have been,
      present, all along?

You mean — that's true?

Interim

Easter trumpets, lilies, clamouring
in a blare of sun
rejoice the few, leave many wondering
what, here, heralds the One

who is one with, distinct from, Him
whose word and its outworking
they tried to seal in stone.
Does love still call him? to long-suffering?

within our death-time? In the morning
pallor of waters, He has come
to vanish — out of human reach, yet waiting
quietly to be known.

Our troubled faces clear to see Him, being
radiantly here, somehow between
familiar days and what's beyond imagining.
We cannot take it in.

Our severed lives are blundering
about in what's been done,
appalled, exultant, sensing
freedom, we seem alone,

but doggedly set out, against a sting
of rain, moved by his plan,
through night and shale-blue dawn, remembering
at least to follow on.

"One Rule of Modesty and Soberness"
(Calvin, on angels, *Institutes* I, xiv, 4)

How to talk about, being mortal,
angels, an angel become
angels?

We want to distract ourselves
    with the sky-thirsting
        saplings of April
or with the so long motionless
pale eggs now wounded with the wobbly
life within them.

Near. In the aftermath, too.
A stupefying brilliance
felled the young guards
yet the mild voice was factual, gentle, with
the laden mourners at a deserted tomb
in the first light of a new era.

Our mortal memory structures
in us what matters — to
bury it, or
re-celebrate so as to
falsify it: we are
made less than the angels, said the ancient
poet, who knew.

    In their remembering it is now:
    wingrush and choiring and joy
    on the shepherds' hill for their
    Shepherd, newborn, nearby, for their
    finding and love.

But now also the darkness
at the third hour has not been able to
obliterate what (except, o woe, to
mortals) is
unthinkable....
Having to know that
darkness is a kind of non-
being for these, an arrest, a stared-at
blank. The resonant
eyes within them must have been
charred, then....

That was, to us humans,
thinkable?

Yes. We do it.
We taunt the promise of hope,
wanting the innocent to
turn and twist like us,
goading him to that end
as though every twist and cruel jibe
he had not already
deliberately absorbed, becoming a
death to be
died to
indeed.

So can a mortal
capable of such violation of such
light, approach the heart of what
that darkness is, to
those pure spirits who are in God's
presence always? who are always

coming and going for
purposes that our heartbreaking
"NO" blacked out, those three long days?

Peter made known that "even
angels long to look
into these things".*
But would the poise of holy nature
be disruptible as is our nature's?

    More likely the
    angel, angels,
    contained, brimmed with, their total pain in
    undemanding quietness.

Not these messengers brought on
the geological convulsion;
nor was the lightning shock
their instantaneous signal.
But unbelief's swift "NO"
wracked earth; mortals resort to
blocking out that way.

    The angel was, the two
    were, merely
    realizing some of the dead man's
    last words, lucidly
    explaining: he will keep his word.
    Expect him.

---

* I Pet. 1:12

Only the breath of dawn-
drenched air moves.

Silence even is music, with
the pressure of *glorias* on
misereres on a threshold of
terrible exaltation.

They found its only release: absorption in
his words, their embassy,
and the new future borning.

It Isn't Really True?

"Attention!
This is not your pilot speaking.

Your pilot is out of control.
Your plane is
crashbound. Attention!
Hear me. Quiet please,
those of you who hear me
and would rather not be hearing me.
Most will not hear or know until
not even risk remains,
only finality.
                    You I am here to direct.
Move quietly to the rear.
Thank you, two, three of you.
Please do as I say, as
you see them doing, you fearful ones.

                    You will all trans-ship.

I will be in control of the
air suction forces on
ejection, and re-boarding.
Yes, in mid-air. You may
trust me: see that round hatchway
low, to your left? It did not
appear till now; the
steward is unaware of it."

                    Roar of blinding blood in the ears,
                    tumult, an interval like freefall
                    and white noise. And

'Look! It's the arrival corridor
of an airport.

        The luggage carousel — I'm
        meeting someone there.
        I know, we left it all ...'
'The flight is in!
It didn't crash!'

        'But we *did* go
        out that hatch ...
        We were looked after, somehow.
        Somehow, don't you feel
        looked after, still?'
'Yes but
"crashbound" the same voice said.'
        'Maybe he meant
        some other kind of ending?'

"Attention!
All passengers from Flight X99
arriving from Dorval,
please reclaim your carry-on
luggage. Report to Airport Lost & Found
before leaving the terminal. *Attention!*"

'Did that other voice
do it bilingually?'
        'No. At least, each heard
        in his own language.
        Some of us were "other".'

FOR THE FUN OF IT

A Seed of History

One brilliantly cold Alberta day
the teacher wrote on the blackboard
'1928' — for the first time. Everything was changing
so that the blue-and-pink map of Canada
still on the wall was a welcome
constant, in the excitement of this
January newness.

We wrote it on our papers
in round big shapes,
Jan., 1928.

The snow outside
glittered like mica-shavings
in the Alberta sunshine.

Word: Russets

Whoever longs for spring to come,
be stayed by winter's hamper-hued
but choicest — russet apples.

Though it still feel iron hard
its seeds are black, its juices sweet.

Aroma? in the seeds?
There is a fragrance of the one-day flower;
later, a tang of fruit; sharper in peel.
But — seeds?

Where else is the aroma hid?
and how much more of good
sensed, anticipated,
or understood.

Shelter?

There's a door in
to the tree,
to the hillside,
to yesterday's home
(they've changed the knocker),
in to the
boathouse-loft snow must have
borne lopsided now
in one corner.

Outdoors, in
under the raftering dusk,
the smoke-red sun
finds an incisive scraggle of
brush on its last
low hill,
signalling time to go
in.

A Kept Secret

One day there flew
from greengold shadows here to those
indigo shadows
deeper among the trees,
in a trice, fanning light,
your wide sky-combing pinions
encompassing, in a breath,
both dark and dazzling.

Each was comprehended and
simply, in equipoise,
contained.

The dark was not
Thomas Hardy's, not
the West's gaunt watershed:
bedaubed everyman, ducking
from any horizon.

Darkness is changed
once it is comprehended; it becomes
knowledge, beyond our reach.

And the flash
stirred by your flight — and gone —
still startles. What does anyone
know of light?

Something to weigh, until
the branches become black
against the amber evening.

Resting On a Dry Log, Park Bench, Boulder

I love to see birds walk.
Oh yes of course, their singing,
their soaring, their
flocking in autumn branches, their
unerring drift down onto a
wire, a tassle of pine:
all these delight.

But that a bird
comes simply among us,
steps as we must (though some,
sandpipers, robins, etc.,
like children bob or run)
touches us.
       They come for seeds
          or crumbs perhaps, a comfortable
touching down we can well understand
although for us to
"consider the birds of the air" in this regard
can be uncomfortable.
          But play is part
          of any living creature's
          energy.

I like to think birds walk
for fun. They trust
another element awhile
as a child wades in snowdrifts.
I have seen delicate patterns
of bird tracks in
deep snow, where only particles of manna

could be there for them, for the drifts
were deep, too deep for grasses, and
there were no shrubs,
and people's footsteps there were none.
Nor were there the faint fanning
traces of wings, on take-off.
Did they jump first, then fly?

Give me no explanations. If a biologist
finds talk of walking birds a
blurring of distinctions, an outsider's
invasion of a territory
with its own necessary laws, and language,
I respect him or her for that,
expecially if this old joke
makes us both smile:

A pigeon was late meeting
a friend at City Hall —
"It was such a fine day," he said,
"I thought I'd walk."

News Item

Today, May 9th
the chestnut trees
pagoda'd in full
seven-fold leaf
out of a blue sky.

Instrumentalists Rehearse

Fishes off on cruises
dream, staring up to sky.

Maple keys let themselves be
sodden and mashed down
into the earth. Their biddable eyes
still towards the trusted
nurturer's, without
any idea what
'fruitful' may turn out to mean
(one papery inch from lofted leafiness!)
— or 'multiply'.

Planets and constellations
dance to like music
not needing to know that
their lost millenia will
shine in a fledgling owl's
eyes in the dark forest deep
deep in the heart of
their fathomless night.

Three Bears

Three polar bears
on a pink ice floe
dance round slow-
ly revolving under
the teal-blue Arc-
tic red-rimmed circle of sky.

Music icicles
picket them round
soundlessly
the dancers three.

They swivel high-
er and higher still
till nobody else was left at all.

JOB: WORD AND ACTION

Confrontation and Resolution, In Job

Proem

Devastation is the seed-bed
for a new era.
Fifteen months of flood waters
recede at last.
Lazarus dies with the saver of lives
summoned, not responding
in time.
John the Baptist grimaces from
Salome's salver.
Jerusalem's stones and golden
ritual vessels
become flesh and blood, and
know it, in
rubble and in
time.

A Book Review

Idle to do this.
Nothing will do
but to r e a d the book.
For one thing, it is
immeasurably better,
and clearer, and
probably more accessible.

Why write about it then?
Because I want to,

to cope with it
in human company.

Words written down
centuries and many centuries
ago in a
faraway land, were properly
special and enigmatic
in some ways
to be studied and pondered. I
thought. And found
the reading put me in
the midst, not as the self I knew
and certainly not by being
manipulated into an other's
identity, but —
on purpose.
I found myself belonging
without suprise, in a new setting.

Anyone who reads this book
risks losing forever any belonging that
he thought defined himself.

Stop here and read the book, if you
want that, not just
a book review.

The Subject

Job was a good man.
His biographer gives a

picture of parental and
political reliability.

When Job refers to his own life
and doings, he elaborates;
the account squares with his three friends'
opinions too.
He was a good man.

(It's not a usual situation
for someone to
define in action what he knows is
perfect polity.)

The Context

If Job did what he said —
and I believe him when he
said it, only because
by then his back was
up against the wall —
if in the dismissive eye
of all the disbelievers, also
facing himself, even then,
he said it,
anyone would believe:

he had not once
failed a hungry man or a
defenceless child or an
abandoned woman or
the stranger at his door.

If he did give what it took
always (and yet
he also said
his table, and all his sons', also his servants'
tables were unfailingly
bountiful — and I believe him),
then was he something like a spring-fed brook
irrigating the places that would be
too dry for growing, otherwise; —
and did that leave him, like
the other wealthy ones
around — and with the help of
sons and servants —
thriving by giving, able
increasingly to raise more crops?

That would have been a
government by the richest, then —
who were to be rewarded
for having done the right thing
always.

The book of Job is no "Utopia" though.

Events

No seeds of the disasters
that struck were in
the having done it well
surely.
        In one night
everything was wiped out.
Pain and revulsion and

indignities
only, remained.

The Reviewer Speculates

Was there a jaundiced eye watching and
hoping perfection somehow would be marred?
Perhaps the followers of his
example, kindly citizens, might
have been inclined, later, to speculate
about some flaw in him
that brought him down.

But they were friends.
They waited
for days for some
evidence, first.

The Issue

A conviction was at stake for
Job — and for his friends.
Job felt it keenly and
for them it mattered too:
to affirm the fairness of
the ethical order. Perhaps they also
felt an obligation to
blame someone — yes, blame Job.
He and his situation
would not fit, otherwise.

Their rock-solid convictions
steadied them in the rough

sea of their friend's
grief, magnificent courage, and
refusal to despair.

His struggle to take it, and
to take it in, they did
recognize — but not the
appalling loneliness.

He listened — for
one word to break
in upon the core of his
desolation. Their
speaking only defined
a special doom he stoutly
denied himself
i.e. that he was quite
alone in a
though baffling and beautiful
yet meaninglessly devastating
homeless wilderness.

The Reviewer Interpolates

Your reviewer had expected
something quite different in the
working out of the story.
Visitors spent days counselling
contrition as a therapy,
or equanimity (from
someone in extremis!) — distance
lends its own perspective.

Surely God would come and
console His child.
After all, it was Job
who, in the first shock,
nonetheless kept his grip
firm on one reality:
the One with all
power was in the end the
only trustworthy one.

He was not consoled.

Was Job being honoured then
for enduring?

Was it that either comfort or
compensation would have seemed ...
patronising?

In any case it only
made sense — read it yourself and
see what you think —
this way, for me, right now:

Wrath Is Felt From Its Source

What was pushing the Other
past patience?
        Of course there is no parallel
        anywhere.
        But a person can
        remember standing at a bedside
        ineffectually and

seeing somebody in dire distress,
who is isolated by it
and fights off isolation, and
gropes for vital contact.
The person keeping vigil
trembles within, knowing
no means but touch, and voice.
These don't get through.
Words evaporate then.

Soliloquy

There is no way
to open my counsel.
I have been close by
knowing ahead that I would have to choose
powerlessness. No
intervening. And would be
unable to explain —
and all because I
trusted your integrity, Job.

But searing is this
wordlessness.

>He was the One to whom
>Job shouted, whispered, always addressing
>the ultimate question.
>Job was tormented to know
>how it could all make sense.

I knew,
but oh, out of Job's range.

*　　*　　*

And so the Lord endured —
His Presence like white sound —
while His child struggled to find foothold
in faith, anticipating
deliverance, when the One
who secures all that holds would heed
and show the way and
finally force his battered
misunderstandings to be gone.

Understanding?

No words but His own
word can be
reliable, or safely used
in speculation.

When he confused their language
at Babel, and the achievements
crumbled, wasn't that
merciful?

Somebody said
(I'm quoting) "There is a
danger that everything, through being misnamed
will be misunderstood", something like that.

I.e. we go on building on our self-
generated constructs, with a self-
referrent valuing. But in a not
self-generated universe.

Is our communal language —
dollars and mega-bytes and so on —
just a few stages past our
Meccano sets?

Hard-won are the words
we need to truly
converse with someone close
and yet mysterious to us.

Impasse

Why can't Job glimpse
the truth of feeling on both sides?
And the sufferer
presses, presses.

> It would be unworthy to
> speak some approximating
> word, not a real answer,
> thus negating your respect
> for the true question. Would you break
> the other's integrity?

No. You plunge him in
terror, and awe:
through indigo ocean currents, among
shelves where coral builds on
coral. To Job's stunned
absorption, teeming creation flashed and,
intricate and monstrous,
its creatures sublimely
untroubled, burned with their being.

Job awoke then to a
newly vivid sense of his littleness.

Someone had after all been
listening to him all through
the times he ranted, through his
desperate appeals. Someone had let
the barriers build up
between you, in pure pain.

It came then.
Job was scathed — although
but briefly — by the wrath.

Whatever Job felt when the voice
stormed at him, any reader of this book
is outraged!

> "Will the one who contends with the Almighty
> correct Him?
> Let him who accuses God
> answer Him!" *
> and
> "Would you discredit My justice
> Would you condemn Me to justify yourself?"**

Restive Interlude

Did you too, reader,
have to put down the book

---

*   40:1
** 40:8

to let your seething settle?

E.g. did you too
ask, Was Job wrong
to cry out,
    "If I have sinned
    how do I injure Thee,
    Thou Watcher of the
    hearts of men?"*

    or, "I call for help but
    Thou dost not answer. I stand up
    to plead, but Thou
    sittest aloof"?**

And then Job listened

even through that storm, intent,
he listened.

The Brief Words of Anger, Over

    That part breaks off. Magenta
    clouds boil away and blanch.
    The thunderer abruptly, but
    wholly encompasses His man:
    plunges him through
    night's plotted skies; then floundering
    light-flooded skies during a March gale;

---

*   7:20
** 3:20-21

vast unvisited snowfields, and
Galapagos's coast.

Then, after those
avalanching wonders,
every creature's every detail was revealed,
a centre of this Other's
acute awareness. Equally.
Prairie crocus or coyote or
seas braiding around Leviathan.

By then Job knew
what it is to be broken and
to be overwhelmed in his littleness by
power, and the glory.

Finis

It ends up not to be
a biography.
Another Presence turns out to be
dominant — yet without Job's
dwindling.
The other is
beyond any biographer.
When He speaks for Himself
word and action are all but identical.

When were they not
identical?